Extreme Trees
And How They Got That Way

by Ellen Lawrence

Consultants:

Melissa Islam, PhD
Associate Director of Research and Head Curator of Gardens' Herbaria
Denver Botanic Gardens

Kimberly Brenneman, PhD
National Institute for Early Education Research, Rutgers University
New Brunswick, New Jersey

BEARPORT
PUBLISHING

New York, New York

Credits

Cover, © James Randklev/Corbis; 2–3, © Jarous/Shutterstock; 3R, © africa924/istockphoto; 4, © Thierry Guinet/Shutterstock; 5, © Don Paulson Photography/Purestock/Alamy; 6, © africa924/istockphoto; 7, © Stefan Huwiler/Imagebroker/FLPA; 7R, © Dr. Morley Read/Shutterstock; 8, © Robert Harrison/Alamy; 9, © James Randklev/Corbis; 9R, © Chris Martin/Alamy; 10, TR, © Mauro Halpern; 10–11, © Jo Crebbin/Shutterstock; 11R, © Michael McMurrough/Alamy; 12, © Dr. Morley Read/Science Photo Library; 12–13, © Vladimir Melnik/Shutterstock; 14–15, © Muriel Hazan/Biosphoto.com; 16–17, © saiko3p/Shutterstock; 18, © Ruth Owen; 19, © Jaime Plaza/Royal Botanic Gardens Sydney; 20, © Public Domain; 21, © Rob McBride/www.treehunter.co.uk; 22, © Dionisvera/Shutterstock, © Perutskyi Petro/Shutterstock, © Andrey Eremin/Shutterstock, © LehaKoK/Shutterstock, © Samoloff/Shutterstock, © jcfmorata/Shutterstock, © Tamara Kulikova/Shutterstock, and © Oleg Mikhaylov/Shutterstock; 23TL, © Jaime Plaza/Royal Botanic Gardens Sydney; 23TC, © Linda Bucklin/Shutterstock; 23TR, © 501room/Shutterstock; 23BL, © apiguide/Shutterstock; 23BC, © Dr. Morley Read/Science Photo Library; 23BR, © Nigel Cattlin/FLPA.

Publisher: Kenn Goin
Editorial Director: Adam Siegel
Creative Director: Spencer Brinker
Design: Emma Randall
Photo Researcher: Ruby Tuesday Books Ltd

Library of Congress Cataloging-in-Publication Data

Lawrence, Ellen, 1967-
  Extreme trees / by Ellen Lawrence.
     pages cm. — (Plant-ology)
  Audience: Age: 7-12.
  Includes bibliographical references and index.
  ISBN-13: 978-1-62724-306-3 (library binding : alk. paper)
  ISBN-10: 1-62724-306-2 (library binding : alk. paper)
  1. Trees—Juvenile literature. 2. Trees—Defenses—Juvenile literature. I. Title.
  QK475.8.L39 2015
  582.16—dc23
                    2014014035

33614059715002

For more information, write to Bearport Publishing Company, Inc., 45 West 21st Street, Suite 3B, New York, New York 10010. Printed in the United States of America.

10 9 8 7 6 5 4 3 2 1

Contents

That's Extreme!

Trees grow in forests, parks, and yards around the world.

They all have roots, trunks, branches, and leaves, but they don't all look the same.

Some trees are extreme.

They might have huge trunks or grow to be super tall.

A giant sequoia (sih-KWOY-uh) tree nicknamed General Sherman has a trunk that is more than 36 feet (11 m) wide.

That's about the same as nine children lying head to toe!

General Sherman Tree

The General Sherman Tree is the heaviest living thing on Earth. Scientists think its enormous trunk and branches weigh 2,000 tons (1,814 metric tons)—the weight of more than 400 elephants!

NORTH AMERICA

The General Sherman Tree

Pacific Ocean

SOUTH AMERICA

Atlantic Ocean

The General Sherman Tree lives in California.

General Sherman Tree

GENERAL SHERMAN

5

Giants of the Rain Forest

Kapok trees are not as thick and heavy as giant sequoias.

In **rain forests** around the world, however, they are the tallest trees.

A kapok tree can grow to be 250 feet (76 m) tall—higher than a 20-story building.

It may grow 13 feet (4 m) in just one year.

The huge tree may also produce up to 4,000 fruits in a year!

Where kapok trees grow

dried kapok fruit

fluffy fiber

seeds

Each piece of fruit from a kapok tree has about 200 seeds inside. The seeds are protected by a fluffy, white, cotton-like fiber. People sometimes use the fiber for stuffing pillows and mattresses.

Look at the way the bottom part of the tree spreads out. How do you think this might help the tree?

(The answer is on page 24.)

kapok tree

7

A Rainbow of Color

At a height of up to 250 feet (76 m), the rainbow gum tree is very tall.

That's not the only extreme thing about it, however.

This tree also has a rainbow-colored trunk.

The bark on the trunk peels off in patches.

When a patch of old bark falls off, there is new green bark underneath.

Over time, the green bark changes to a different color, such as red, orange, or purple.

rainbow gum tree

Bark is a tough protective covering that grows on a tree's trunk and branches. It helps keep a tree from being harmed by rain, snow, or hot sun, and from being eaten by animals.

old bark

new bark

Rainbow gum trees grow in many countries around the world. They grow where the weather is warm all year long.

Some trees have more than tough bark to protect their trunks from animals. In what other way might a tree protect its trunk?

9

Spiky Trunks

Some trees have trunks that are covered with prickles or thorns.

Silk floss trees and honey locust trees both have spiky trunks.

The sharp spikes stop animals from eating the trees.

Honey locust trees have thorns that can grow to be six inches (15 cm) long.

In the past, people used the hard, sharp thorns as nails and needles.

honey locust tree thorns

silk floss tree

■ Where honey locust trees grow

■ Where silk floss trees grow

NORTH AMERICA

Atlantic Ocean

Pacific Ocean

SOUTH AMERICA

N W E S

silk floss tree trunk

prickles

Some silk floss trees grow in hot, dry places where not much rain falls. When it does rain, the trees can store water in their prickles for dry times.

11

Dripping Dragon's Blood

Some trees are extreme because of what's inside them.

If the trunk of a dragon's blood tree is cut, a thick red liquid oozes out.

The sticky liquid isn't really blood, of course.

Instead, it is a substance called **resin**.

Many trees leak resin if they are cut or damaged.

The resin seals up the damaged wood and keeps insects from getting inside and harming the tree.

resin

People use the resin of dragon's blood trees as paint to decorate houses and pottery. People also use it on cuts and scratches on their skin to stop infections.

dragon's blood tree

EUROPE

ASIA

AFRICA

Socotra

Atlantic
Ocean

Indian
Ocean

N
W E
S

Dragon's blood trees grow
on an island in the Indian
Ocean called Socotra.

13

Danger—Deadly Poison!

The bottle tree is extreme because it is very poisonous.

Where is its deadly poison found?

It is in the **sap**.

This liquid carries food and water through the tree.

In the past, hunters used bottle tree sap to poison the tips of their arrows.

AFRICA

Atlantic Ocean

Indian Ocean

N
W   E
S

Where bottle trees grow

Bottle trees grow in dry deserts. When it rains, a bottle tree stores a huge amount of water in its trunk. This makes the tree's trunk swell up into a bulging, bottle-like shape.

bottle tree

trunk

The bottle tree gets its name from its strange shape. Try making up a new name that describes the tree.

Spreading Banyan Trees

Most trees have roots that grow down from their trunks and into the ground.

A banyan tree, however, sprouts roots from its branches.

The roots grow down through the air and into the soil.

As the years pass, they become thick and woody.

The roots make the tree look as if it has lots of trunks!

The world's largest banyan tree grows in India. By growing branches from its roots, it has spread over an area that's nearly as big as three football fields. The giant tree looks like a forest!

branch

roots growing down from branches

banyan tree

ASIA

Pacific Ocean

AFRICA

N

W E

S

Indian Ocean

Where banyan trees grow

A Prehistoric Tree

The wollemi (WAWL-uhm-eye) pine tree is not huge, spiky, or poisonous—but it is very special.

This kind of tree was living on Earth at the time of the dinosaurs.

For a long time, though, scientists thought the trees were **extinct**—just like the dinosaurs.

They believed that only **fossils** of the trees remained.

Then, in 1994, some wollemi pines were found growing in a forest in Australia.

It was an amazing discovery—almost like finding some dinosaurs hidden away in a forest!

wollemi pine trees

Scientists have found a fossil that shows **ancestors** of today's wollemi pines existed about 90 million years ago.

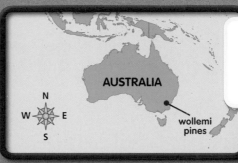

This map shows where in Australia the wollemi pines were found in 1994.

AUSTRALIA

wollemi pines

fossil

wollemi pine tree branch

The Chapel Oak

Oak trees are large trees with thick trunks and branches.

In France, there is an oak tree that's big enough to contain two small chapels!

One of these tiny churches is at the bottom of the tree's trunk.

The other is higher up and can be reached by a staircase.

The chapels were built in 1696, and people still visit them today.

The oak tree is named the Chapel Oak. It is between 800 and 1,000 years old.

the Chapel Oak

This map shows where in France the Chapel Oak grows.

an entrance to the Chapel Oak

21

Science Lab

Be a Tree Detective

When you are in your backyard, on the street, or in a park or forest, search for trees and things that came from trees.

See how many of the things on this page you can find.

Bring a notebook and pencil or a camera with you. Draw or photograph what you find.

acorns from an oak tree

a tree with an unusual shape

a tree with a thick trunk

a tree with patterned or colorful bark

a cone from a tree

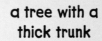

a very tall tree

a leaf with an unusual shape, color, or pattern

22

Science Words

ancestors (AN-sess-turz) people, animals, or plants that lived a long time ago, but have relatives alive today

extinct (ek-STINGKT) when a kind of plant or animal has died out, and there are no more of its kind anywhere on Earth

fossils (FOSS-uhlz) what is left of plants or animals that lived long ago

rain forests (RAYN FOR-ists) places where many trees and other plants grow and lots of rain falls

resin (REZ-in) a thick, sticky liquid inside the trunk and branches of some trees that seals up the bark if it gets damaged

sap (SAP) a liquid that flows through a plant and carries water and food for the plant

Index

Read More

Cherry, Lynne. *The Great Kapok Tree: A Tale of the Amazon Rain Forest.* Orlando, FL: First Voyager Books (2000).

Owen, Ruth. *Science and Craft Projects with Trees and Leaves (Get Crafty Outdoors).* New York: Rosen (2013).

Tagliaferro, Linda. *The Life Cycle of an Oak Tree (Pebble Plus).* North Mankato, MN: Capstone (2007).

Learn More Online

To learn more about extreme trees, visit
www.bearportpublishing.com/Plant-ology

About the Author

Ellen Lawrence lives in the United Kingdom. Her favorite books to write are those about nature and animals. In fact, the first book Ellen bought for herself, when she was six years old, was the story of a gorilla named Patty Cake that was born in New York's Central Park Zoo.

Answers

Page 7: Many huge rain forest trees grow parts called buttress roots. *Buttress* means "to support." These roots grow above the ground and spread out at the bottom of a tree's trunk. They help support the giant tree and keep it from falling over.